W9-CDO-279 2008

THE FEDERAL BUREAU OF INVESTIGATION

THE U.S. GOVERNMENT
HOW IT WORKS

★ ★ ★

THE CENTRAL INTELLIGENCE AGENCY
THE DEPARTMENT OF HOMELAND SECURITY
THE FEDERAL BUREAU OF INVESTIGATION
THE HOUSE OF REPRESENTATIVES
THE PRESIDENCY
THE SENATE
THE SUPREME COURT

THE U.S. GOVERNMENT
HOW IT WORKS

THE FEDERAL BUREAU OF INVESTIGATION

HEATHER LEHR WAGNER

CHELSEA HOUSE
PUBLISHERS
An imprint of Infobase Publishing

The Federal Bureau of Investigation

Chelsea House
An imprint of Infobase Publishing
132 West 31st Street
New York, NY 10001

ISBN-10: 0-7910-9281-X
ISBN-13: 978-0-7910-9281-1

Library of Congress Cataloging-in-Publication Data
Wagner, Heather Lehr.
  The Federal Bureau of Investigation / Heather Lehr Wagner.
      p. cm. — (The U.S. government: how it works)
  Includes bibliographical references and index.
  ISBN 0-7910-9281-X (hardcover)
  1. United States. Federal Bureau of Investigation—Juvenile literature.
  2. Criminal investigation—United States—Juvenile literature. I. Title. II. Series.

  HV8144.F43W34 2007
  363.250973—dc22
                                    2006028393

Series design by James Scotto-Lavino
Cover design by Ben Peterson

Printed in the United States of America

Bang FOF 10 9 8 7 6 5 4 3 2 1

This book is printed on acid-free paper.

All links and Web addresses were checked and verified to be correct at the time of publication. Because of the dynamic nature of the Web, some addresses and links may have changed since publication and may no longer be valid.

CONTENTS

1

An Attempt
at Sabotage

It was nearly midnight on June 13, 1942. The United States had entered World War II some six months earlier, after the bombing of Pearl Harbor. The nation's leading law enforcement agency, the Federal Bureau of Investigation (FBI), was aware that spies from Japan, Germany, or Italy—America's enemies in World War II— might try to bring the conflict to American soil. A list of Japanese, German, and Italian aliens living in the United States had been compiled. The FBI's director, J. Edgar Hoover, ordered FBI agents to review telegraph and cable messages to certain countries before they were sent and to read mail being sent to and from the German and Japanese embassies. Security was increased at defense plants and important industrial sites.

On that June night, a 21-year-old Coast Guards-man named John Cullen left the Coast Guard station at Amagansett, Long Island, on a routine midnight beach patrol. He was alone and armed only with a flashlight. As he walked along the beach, he noticed four men in the water, struggling with a large raft. He approached them and asked what they were doing. They replied that they were fishermen who had become lost in the fog. Then, one of the men said something in German.

Cullen was alarmed. He was by himself, without a weapon, and at least four men were confronting him. One of the men offered him a bribe of $260 and told him to forget what he had seen. Cullen pretended to accept the bribe. He took the money, hurried back to the Coast Guard station, and reported what had happened. He led a small team back to the place on the beach where he had confronted the "fishermen," but they had disappeared. In the distance, the Coast Guardsmen could hear the sound of an engine rumbling in the foggy darkness.

When dawn came, the Coast Guardsmen returned to the spot on the beach and searched the area thoroughly. They spotted footprints in the sand and followed them to the dunes. There, buried in the sand, they found explo-sives, timing devices, and German military uniforms.

The four men who had claimed to be fishermen were ac-tually German agents who had been trained in the art of sabotage. Their names were George Dasch, Ernest Burger, Heinrich Heinck, and Richard Quirin. They had all been born in Germany and had all spent part of their lives in

An FBI poster from 1942 warned against spies and saboteurs during World War II. That year, the Federal Bureau of Investigation captured eight German agents who were sent to the United States to attack manufacturing plants and transportation facilities.

the United States. They were fluent in American English, familiar with American customs, and could easily blend into American society.

The men had spent three weeks at a special training school on a private estate near Berlin, Germany, learning how to manufacture and use explosives, incendiary material, and various timing devices. They were taught different ways to use an abrasive material to destroy machines and engines. They learned where an explosive should be placed on a bridge or in a factory to create the maximum damage. They were taken to aluminum and magnesium plants, railroads, canals, and river locks in Germany and shown where the most vulnerable places in these facilities would be. They were given new identities with a detailed history—new lives were created for them and supported by phony birth certificates, driver's licenses, and Social Security cards.

At the school was a second team of German agents, also being trained in preparation for sabotage on American soil. George Dasch had been appointed the head of the first team. Their targets, once they reached the United States, were the Aluminum Company of America plant in Alcoa, Tennessee; an aluminum plant in East St. Louis, Illinois; the Cryolite plant in Philadelphia, Pennsylvania; and the locks on the Ohio River from Pittsburgh, Pennsylvania, to Louisville, Kentucky. Dasch and his team were to enter the United States near New York. The second team would enter in Florida and focus on railroad sabotage, placing explosives at Pennsylvania Station in Newark,

New Jersey, and at various facilities of the Chesapeake and Ohio Railroad. They were also to blow up a portion of the Hell Gate railroad bridge that spanned the East River in New York City.

Both teams were to make it clear that sabotage was responsible for these disasters. The Germans did not want their efforts to appear accidental. Instead, they were to demonstrate that American railroads and industries were being targeted, to create an atmosphere of fear and panic in the American public while also hampering rail shipments and light-metal production.

The teams carried with them four waterproof cases containing explosives, bombs disguised to look like large pieces of coal, a variety of fuses, detonators and primers, and chemical and mechanical timing devices. The plan was for these materials to last two years, during which time the saboteurs would create chaos and panic across the United States.

To cover the expenses of their mission, the German agents were given a large amount of American money. Each team leader was given $50,000 as a general fund, plus another $20,000 to be divided equally among the men in the team. Each individual saboteur was given $4,000 in a money belt, and $400 in small bills to be used immediately upon landing in the United States.

The agents dressed in German uniforms for the initial landing. This was done in case of capture, so that they would be treated as prisoners of war rather than spies if they were discovered before they could begin their mission. They had also been supplied with American clothing, which Dasch and his men had just put on before their encounter with Cullen.

After Cullen left them, they buried their cases of supplies and headed for the nearest train station, where they caught the first train for New York City. The four men split into pairs. Dasch and Burger headed for one hotel, Heinck and Quirin for another.

CAPTURING THE ENEMY

It was not until 12 hours after the landing on Long Island that the Federal Bureau of Investigation was alerted that German spies might have slipped into the United States. A telephone call to the New York office of the FBI requested that an agent come to the Coast Guard captain's office. There, the cases of sabotage equipment were produced, and Cullen once again told his story.

Hoover, the FBI director, was quickly told of the incident. Hoover determined that the best course of action was not to inform the public. A public announcement that German spies had landed on American shores would cause panic, he felt, and would also alert the saboteurs that their plot had been uncovered.

The decision was a risky one. An alerted public might be able to report suspicious activity and help with the capture of the saboteurs. Hoover, though, was confident that the FBI would be able to discover and capture the men, and he wanted to keep their presence in the United States secret until they were in FBI custody.

Hoover immediately ordered FBI agents to begin a comprehensive search for the German agents. As investigators frantically began the hunt, Dasch and Burger had a long discussion in their New York hotel that would make the hunt much easier. Dasch, who had lived in the United States for more than 20 years before he returned to Germany and was recruited as an agent, was having a change of heart. The confrontation with Cullen had shaken him. He knew that the mission's success depended upon extraordinary luck and that it was highly unlikely he would return to Germany alive. Capture in the United States would probably mean he would receive the death penalty.

Dasch told his partner that he was considering calling off the mission and alerting the FBI. He warned Burger that, if he tried to stop him, he would push Burger out of the hotel window. Burger replied that he had never intended to carry out the sabotage. Instead, he had planned to slip away with the money they had been given to carry out the mission.

That night, Dasch placed a call to the FBI's New York office. He told the agent who answered that he wanted to meet with Hoover. Both the agent and his supervisor decided that the call was a prank or that the caller was mentally disturbed, and did nothing further.

Dasch, though, was firmly committed to turning himself in to the FBI, specifically to Hoover. He traveled to Washington, D.C., checked in to the Mayflower Hotel and again tried to phone Hoover. He was transferred several times before he ended up speaking with the head of the

FBI's Domestic Intelligence Division and then with the Sabotage Unit. The connection was finally made between Dasch's call and the landing on Long Island, and two FBI agents were swiftly sent to pick up Dasch at his hotel.

For days, Dasch was interrogated, and he provided the FBI with detailed information about his training in sabotage and the planned targets. He gave the agents information about German submarine capabilities, war production, and secret codes. He told them of the second team, scheduled to land on Ponte Vedra Beach near Jacksonville, Florida, and reported that additional teams were scheduled to land every six weeks to detonate bombs in public places and spark terror and fear in the United States.

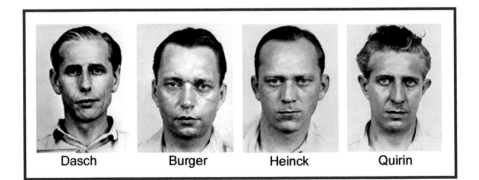

Dasch   Burger   Heinck   Quirin

Four of the German saboteurs caught by the FBI were *(from left)* George Dasch, Ernest Burger, Heinrich Heinck, and Richard Quirin. They landed on a beach on Long Island, New York, in June 1942 equipped with explosives. Soon after, Dasch had a change of heart about the mission and surrendered to the FBI.

FBI agents arrested Heinck, Quirin, and Burger in New York on June 20, 1942. The second group of saboteurs had successfully landed undetected in Florida, staying for some time in Jacksonville before dispersing to different parts of the United States. Alerted to their presence by Dasch, FBI agents arrested two of the men in New York on June 24 and the others in Chicago on June 27.

News that the FBI had captured eight German "spies," who had traveled by submarine to U.S. beaches, electrified the nation. It was a great victory for the FBI, and for its director. The fact that Dasch turned himself in was not widely known. That this case, like many others, was solved because of a tip from someone involved in the plot should not be seen as a weakness of the FBI. Luck would play a role in many of the high-profile cases the FBI would solve throughout its history. Also, in the case of Dasch, it was the reputation of the FBI that caused him to insist on surrendering to that organization, rather than any other.

Perhaps the most important fact of the case is this: Never again did German saboteurs try to land on American soil. On November 29, 1944, when two German spies debarked from a U-boat off the coast of Maine, the FBI swiftly discovered and seized them.

FEDERAL LAW ENFORCEMENT

The FBI today defines its mission in clear terms: to protect and defend the United States against terrorist and foreign intelligence threats, to uphold and enforce the

FBI PRIORITIES

On the Web site of the Federal Bureau of Investigation, the agency outlines its priorities. The section on the Web site (which is found at www.fbi.gov/priorities/priorities.htm) states:

In executing the following priorities, we will produce and use intelligence to protect the nation from threats and to bring to justice those who violate the law.

1. Protect the United States from terrorist attack.
2. Protect the United States against foreign intelligence operations and espionage.
3. Protect the United States against cyber-based attacks and high-technology crimes.
4. Combat public corruption at all levels.
5. Protect civil rights.
6. Combat transnational and national criminal organizations and enterprises.
7. Combat major white-collar crime.
8. Combat significant violent crime.
9. Support federal, state, county, municipal, and international partners.
10. Upgrade technology to successfully perform the FBI's mission.

criminal laws of the United States, and to provide leadership and criminal justice services to federal, state, municipal, and international agencies and partners. When the organization now known as the Federal Bureau of Investigation began nearly 100 years ago, however, it was as a small team of permanent investigators who were to report to the Department of Justice and whose mission was believed to be short-lived. Initially, these investigators focused on antitrust cases, land fraud, and copyright violations. It was not until the United States entered World War I in April 1917 that the FBI's mandate would expand to include espionage, sabotage, and antigovernment activity. At the time, the FBI's personnel numbered a mere 300.

Today, more than 30,000 people work for the FBI. The history of the bureau mirrors the important political events of the United States in the twentieth and twenty-first centuries. The kidnapping of famed aviator Charles Lindbergh's infant son in 1932 led to the passage of the Federal Kidnapping Act, enabling the FBI to investigate kidnappings that crossed state borders. The 1933 Kansas City Massacre led to the passage of crime bills that equipped the FBI to make arrests and to carry weapons.

The rise of gangsters like Baby Face Nelson and John Dillinger in the 1930s brought new public attention to the crime-fighting activities of FBI agents, nicknamed "G-Men," giving them a glamorous and heroic reputation. From providing security for the United States from foreign agents during World War II and the Cold War to investigating civil rights violations and organized crime to combating domestic and international terrorism, the FBI's mandate has grown steadily over time. Throughout nearly half of its history, a single man—J. Edgar Hoover—served as its director, shaping its focus and transforming it into one of the government's most powerful agencies. There have been great successes and embarrassing failures.

In *My FBI*, former FBI Director Louis J. Freeh notes the challenges of overseeing an organization as vast as the FBI:

> Think of yourself as running a company that produces everything from applesauce to zippers; a company with 535 members on its board of directors, three-quarters of whom must run for re-election every two years; then imagine yourself reporting as CEO up through a chain of command with a dozen different agendas, under constant media scrutiny, knowing that every memorandum, every piece of paper, every smallest secret is in constant danger of being leaked. And then give your employees weapons and send them out to perform the country's most dangerous work. Give yourself a firearm, too, and work like a dog from sunup to well after sundown, and you'll have some idea of what the FBI director's job is like.

The story of the FBI begins with 34 agents, some of them Secret Service agents borrowed from the Treasury Department. Crime in those early days of the twentieth century was largely a local matter, with the exception of a few "special" crimes. To investigate these "special" crimes, these 34 "special agents" were appointed by the U.S. attorney general. Because Congress was worried about any attempt to create a so-called national police force, these special agents could not make an arrest or carry a weapon. It is with this small group of agents that the Federal Bureau of Investigation began.

2

SPECIAL AGENTS

The Federal Bureau of Investigation had very humble beginnings. The agency that today employs more than 30,000 people began in 1908 with a mere 34 "special agents," named because of the so-called special crimes they were charged with investigating. These agents were hired by Attorney General Charles J. Bonaparte to investigate violations of federal banking, postal, and antitrust laws, as well as any criminal acts against the federal government. This group, still without a name, sparked tremendous concern among members of Congress, who warned of the dangers of creating a "secret police force" that, they cautioned, would be used to spy on ordinary Americans. Crime was considered to be a local matter early in the twentieth century, a problem for local or state police forces to handle.

Attorney General Bonaparte, however, argued that his detectives, attached to the Justice Department, would

U.S. Attorney General Charles J. Bonaparte *(above)* hired 34 "special agents" in 1908 to investigate violations of federal banking, postal, and antitrust laws. This team of agents was the beginning of the Federal Bureau of Investigation. At the time, the idea of a "national police force" caused some trepidation.

perform a vital service. He offered to be personally responsible—subject to impeachment—if his detectives should stray beyond their assigned duties. Congress added further restrictions—the agents were not allowed to make arrests or carry any firearms.

By March 1909, the special agents who made up the Justice Department's investigative division were known as the Bureau of Investigation. The bureau's earliest cases involved interstate crimes and required agents to be stationed in Washington, D.C., as well as in the nation's other largest cities. This increasing focus on a nationwide presence reflected changes in American society. In the early part of the twentieth century, Americans were moving from rural areas to the cities. More and more immigrants were arriving in the United States. The introduction of the automobile made transportation easier. With all of these changes, concern was growing that local police departments would be unable to handle criminals who might cross state lines.

The 1919 Dyer Act, or National Motor Vehicle Theft Act, helped ensure the rise of the bureau's influence. The Dyer Act authorized the bureau to investigate whenever stolen automobiles were taken from one state to another. As more cars were sold, more were also stolen. Agents, acting on their own and with the help of the local police, were able to recover many cars and arrest those involved in their theft. These impressive arrest and recovery statistics provided solid proof that a federal "police force" was a necessity. The act also gave the bureau a tool with which to investigate criminals who evaded local authorities by crossing state lines.

THE UNITED STATES AT WAR

During the early part of the twentieth century, the bureau's presence was felt in other ways, as well. When the United States entered World War I in 1917, the federal government turned to the Justice Department's agents to help prevent domestic protests from weakening the war effort. The government needed to build up its military and increase spending to cover war costs. Protesters opposing U.S. involvement in the war, which pitted Great Britain, France, and Russia against the Central Powers of Germany and Austria-Hungary, were making it difficult for the government to pursue its policies. There was also concern that Americans or immigrants might be recruited to serve as spies.

A series of acts passed in 1917 and 1918 created further scope for investigations by the bureau. The Espionage Act made it a crime to steal government secrets to help foreign powers. Under the act, it also became a crime to make any verbal or written statement that in some way would "interfere with the operation or success of the military or naval forces of the U.S. or to promote the success of its enemies," cause military personnel to refuse to perform their duties, or prevent the military from recruiting.

The Selective Service Act of 1917 required American men ages 21 to 30 to register to be drafted. The Sedition Act of 1918 forbade any spoken or written "disloyal, profane, scurrilous, or abusive language" critical of the U.S. government. The Immigration Act of 1918 led to the deportation of any immigrants who were members of revolutionary or violent organizations.

These laws equipped the bureau to investigate and arrest many pro-German and pro-Irish activists, members of labor unions, and members of the Socialist and Communist parties. As World War I ended, however, the bureau's investigations into so-called radical groups did not cease. Concern about increasing protests by black Americans prompted the bureau to investigate the NAACP and black activist Marcus Garvey. Much of what the bureau uncovered about union, Communist, and other activist groups was shared with business and political leaders, who used the information to break up unions and ensure their own political advantage.

When it was discovered a few years later that bureau agents had been investigating Democratic Senators Burton Wheeler and Thomas Walsh, both from Montana—tapping their phones, reading their mail, and breaking into their offices to hunt for incriminating information—the worst fears of those who had opposed the creation of a "national police force" seemed to be realized. As part of the Teapot Dome scandal (1923–1924), Wheeler and Walsh were leading a Senate investigation of Secretary of the Interior Albert Fall, who (it was suggested) might have been bribed into leasing oil reserves in Teapot Dome, Wyoming, and Elk Hills, California, without competitive bidding.

The bureau's activities—and their efforts to monitor congressional critics of President Warren G. Harding and his administration—led to a scandal, resulting in the resignation of the attorney general, Harry M. Daugherty, and the firing of the bureau director.

RESTORING CONFIDENCE

New guidelines were issued to clarify and limit the bureau's role. Wiretapping was banned, investigations were strictly limited to the enforcement of federal laws, and the bureau was to focus on criminal actions, not political opinions or protests.

J. Edgar Hoover, a 29-year-old lawyer who had been the bureau's assistant director responsible for overseeing its General Intelligence Division, was named the director of the revamped bureau. Hoover was a strict and hard worker who, it was thought, would transform the bureau into a more disciplined organization. Hoover immediately began to fire political appointees and those who did not meet his strict criteria. New hiring policies were developed to transform the bureau into a more professional organization, and a training school for new agents was created. Originally located in New York, the school moved to Washington, D.C., in 1928 and then to a new facility in Quantico, Virginia, in 1972.

Hoover was determined to elevate his agents to a position of respect. Agents had to follow strict dress codes, wearing dark suits, ties, white shirts, and snap-brimmed hats. Their hair was to be neat and cut conservatively; their shoes were always to be shined.

Office procedures were standardized under Hoover. A printed form was to be used for all interviews. Letters were checked for spelling and approved before being sent out. Field offices were all organized under a similar system, with

J. Edgar Hoover is seen in a 1936 FBI documentary, *You Can't Get Away With It*. Hoover became director of the FBI in 1924, and he would lead the agency until his death in 1972.

a single special agent in charge. Each special agent in charge was made personally responsible for his field office, and any mistakes made by anyone in the office became the responsibility of the special agent in charge, as well. This standardization meant that an agent could walk into any field office and find the same structure, the same dress code, the same procedures, and the same forms to be completed.

Hoover knew that there was still a deep suspicion about the competitive threat that the bureau might pose to state police forces. To gain support from local law enforcement, he established a national Fingerprint Division in 1924, which provided a database for the local police to use to identify criminals who were guilty of crimes in other states. In 1932, he established a Crime Laboratory, which used new technology to identify suspects and their standard methods of committing a crime. This marked the beginning of an important era for the bureau—the use of technology to solve crimes. Local police forces did not have the resources to acquire new technology, and they became increasingly dependent on the bureau to supply them with access to it as needed.

THE G-MAN

In the 1930s, the rise of gangsters and a number of highly publicized bank robberies and kidnappings made it clear that the state and local police were unable to protect the public completely. More than simply coordinating and providing a database, the bureau was needed to help address the rise in crime. From 1932 to 1939, personnel in

An investigator conducts work in the FBI Laboratory, in a photo from 1944. J. Edgar Hoover opened the laboratory in 1932 as the agency began to use technology to solve crimes. The laboratory also allowed the FBI to establish closer ties to local police authorities, who did not have the resources to obtain such technology.

the bureau more than doubled from 801 (including 388 agents) to 1,912 (including 713 agents), according to *The FBI: A Comprehensive Reference Guide.*

One of the most famous of these very public crimes was the kidnapping of the infant son of the famous aviator Charles Lindbergh in 1932. The baby was taken from the Lindbergh home in New Jersey, and a ransom of $50,000 was demanded in exchange for information about where the baby could be found. The Lindberghs paid the ransom, but the information they received turned out to be false. More than two months passed before the baby's body was recovered in a shallow grave near the Lindbergh home.

At the time, kidnapping was not a federal crime. The state and local police tried to solve the case. Feverish newspaper headlines reminded the public that the person responsible for the Lindbergh kidnapping was still at large. After more than a year had passed, President Franklin D. Roosevelt ordered the bureau to take over the investigation. It was not until the fall of 1934 that unemployed carpenter Bruno Hauptmann was identified as the kidnapper. He was ultimately convicted of the kidnapping and murder of the Lindbergh baby and executed in 1936.

The kidnapping of the Lindbergh baby formed—at least in the public's eye—part of a nationwide spree that underscored the sense that crime was now a national concern, not a local one. Gangsters became famous for their crimes and for their nicknames, including Charles "Pretty Boy" Floyd, George "Machine Gun" Kelly, "Baby Face" Nelson, and "Handsome" John Dillinger.

The Dillinger case offers a useful illustration of yet another instance when the bureau was called in after local law enforcement efforts had failed. Dillinger robbed 10 banks in five states from May 1933 to July 1934. Dillinger was captured once but escaped from jail. In a particularly embarrassing incident for local law enforcement officials, he even successfully robbed a police station in Indiana, taking weapons and ammunition. At the time of Dillinger's crime spree, bank robbery was not a federal offense, but it was clear that the bureau needed to be involved in his capture. Bureau agents decided to charge Dillinger with violating the Dyer Act, since he had crossed state lines in a stolen car. Dillinger was ultimately shot and killed by bureau agents in 1934

In the early 1930s, John Dillinger was considered "Public Enemy No. 1." Dillinger had robbed 10 banks in a little more than a year, and the FBI was called in after efforts by local authorities to capture him failed. FBI agents shot and killed Dillinger in 1934 outside a movie theater in Chicago.

FROM INVESTIGATIVE DIVISION TO FBI ★ ★

The investigative unit of the Justice Department has grown and experienced several name changes on its way to becoming the modern FBI:

Official name	Date given
Unit's formation—no official name	July 26, 1908
Bureau of Investigation	March 16, 1909
United States Bureau of Investigation	July 1, 1932
Division of Investigation	August 10, 1933
Federal Bureau of Investigation	July 1, 1935

outside a movie theater in Chicago. Bureau agents also apprehended Kelly, Nelson, and Floyd.

Given the publicity attached to the Lindbergh and Dillinger cases, President Roosevelt decided that the time had come to expand the role that the federal government played in law enforcement. In 1933 and 1934, legislation expanded federal crimes to include kidnapping, bank robbery, extortion (intimidating someone into providing information or money), and transporting stolen property across state lines. Agents were given the right to carry firearms and make arrests. The bureau's success at apprehending such infamous criminals as Nelson and Floyd had earned its agents the nickname "G-Men" (for government men). Previously they had been known as "the feds."

In 1935, the Bureau of Investigation was given a new name to reflect its role. On July 1, 1935, it officially became the Federal Bureau of Investigation.

3

An Independent
Agency

By the late 1930s, the Federal Bureau of Investigation's focus had shifted from apprehending gangsters to apprehending so-called subversive elements in American society. Communist, Fascist, and Socialist groups had successfully risen to power in Europe; the administration of President Franklin D. Roosevelt was concerned that the same groups might successfully challenge the political system in the United States.

Roosevelt approached J. Edgar Hoover, the FBI director, authorizing him to undertake counterespionage operations to survey organizations and individuals affiliated with Communist, Fascist, and Socialist groups. These operations were done without the authorization of the Justice Department, gradually setting the stage for the FBI to move out from under the direct supervision of the attorney general and into a more independent role. The FBI's activities now fell into two broad areas—investigations of specific, clearly defined criminal activities, and intelligence operations against groups whose actions, while not violating a specific federal law, might be thought to pose a threat to the president's policies or decisions.

These activities increased in 1939, when World War II began and concerns increased about the influence and activities of American Fascists and Communists. By May 1940, the White House was sending to the FBI the names of people who had written to protest President Roosevelt's foreign policies, and the FBI was investigating these individuals and providing the White House with reports of their activities. This could hardly be categorized as "counterespionage"—many of these individuals had simply written a letter or sent a telegraph to express their hope that the United States would remain neutral in the war that was sweeping over Europe. Even journalists and publishers of conservative newspapers critical of Roosevelt were subject to FBI surveillance.

The expanded FBI authority did result in some successful counterespionage activities to thwart German efforts at sabotage on American soil. The FBI's efforts at counterespionage continued throughout World War II and afterward into the Cold War era. The Cold War refers to the period in which the United States viewed the Soviet Union as an enemy and formed policies based on the idea of containing this perceived threat. Although the two nations did not engage in direct military conflict, the FBI focused its efforts on carefully monitoring American Communists and those who might try to change policy to the Soviet advantage.

Because the Soviet threat was viewed to be of over-whelming concern, the FBI's focus and energy was direct-ed principally on domestic security and espionage, rather than criminal investigation. FBI investigations focused not only on those directly involved in policymaking, but also on artists, writers, college professors, and journalists, those who were thought to be in a position to influence oth-ers. During the 1950s, the FBI did successfully uncover several Soviet spies, including Rudolf Abel (arrested in 1957) and Kaarlo Tuomi (apprehended in 1958 and turned into a double agent).

PROTESTS AND POLITICS

By the 1960s, it was not simply Communist groups that supposedly posed a threat to America's domestic poli-cymaking. Numerous organizations had formed to pro-test government policies. Women's groups sought greater rights; black Americans protested racial injustice; student groups formed to protest American involvement in the Vietnam War. Other issues that sparked protest groups included nuclear weapons testing, the arms race, and U.S. policy toward Cuba.

The FBI became involved in the surveillance of all these groups, at first because of the claimed Communist infiltra-tion of these organizations and then later because of the

FBI Director J. Edgar Hoover *(center)* attended a White House meeting in February 1961 with President John F. Kennedy *(left)* and Attorney General Robert Kennedy. During Kennedy's presidency, the relationship between Hoover and the White House became more distant.

perceived threat they posed to domestic security. As the groups became more militant, FBI agents were more directly involved in efforts to stop their activities. Agents targeted for surveillance not only the white supremacist organization the Ku Klux Klan and black activist groups like the Black Panthers, but also more peaceful protest groups like the Southern Christian Leadership Conference and Clergy and Laity Concerned About Vietnam. Student protests on American college campuses also sparked FBI involvement.

Under President John F. Kennedy, the relationship between Hoover and the White House cooled slightly. Kennedy's brother, Robert Kennedy, served as the U.S. attorney general, and much of the intelligence that the FBI provided to President Kennedy was a result of specific requests from the White House or the attorney general. Robert Kennedy gave special attention to organized crime, and FBI efforts were in large part concentrated on convicting suspected leaders of organized crime. Because there was no obvious paper trail to convict these crime leaders, wiretapping and bugs were the best possible sources for information. Attorney General Kennedy led an effort to persuade Congress to legalize wiretapping, without success. Not until the late 1960s did Congress agree to expand the federal government's powers in the area of law enforcement, leading to passage of the Omnibus Crime Control and Safe Streets (OCCSS) Act of 1968 and the Racketeer Influenced and Corrupt Organization (RICO) Act of 1970.

Under OCCSS, federal agents working on criminal investigations were authorized to use wiretaps and bugs, subject to court-approved warrants. Under RICO, it became illegal to use a legitimate business to conduct an illegal activity and to acquire or operate a business financed by illegal activities. These laws enabled the FBI to become much more proactive in the fight against organized crime.

A TIME OF SCANDAL

During Attorney General Kennedy's tenure, the FBI began its surveillance of the headquarters of the Southern

Christian Leadership Conference and the home of Martin Luther King, Jr. For some time, Hoover and the FBI had been criticized for not taking a more aggressive role in the civil rights movement, particularly for not protecting civil rights activists when protests grew violent. Hoover's argument was that, since no federal laws were being violated, the FBI lacked jurisdiction to become involved, as its role was not to preserve the peace but to investigate federal crimes. Some suggested that, because FBI agents and local law enforcement officials worked cooperatively to solve crimes, the FBI lacked objectivity when conflicts arose between local police officers and civil rights activists. Others charged that Hoover did not understand or sympathize with those who led the civil rights movement.

It is certainly clear that Hoover, offended by Martin Luther King, Jr.'s criticism of the FBI, responded by launching an extensive surveillance campaign against King. Initially, Hoover told the Kennedy administration that members of King's inner circle were linked to the U.S. Communist Party, thus justifying the surveillance. Claiming that its surveillance could prevent the Communists from infiltrating the civil rights movement, the FBI began to wiretap King's offices at the SCLC and his home in Atlanta. A few months later, the FBI began to plant microphones in hotel and motel rooms where King was staying. This action was taken without Attorney General Kennedy's knowledge, done as part of a campaign to weaken King's influence and embarrass him. FBI efforts to discredit King continued until his assassination in 1968.

Under President Lyndon B. Johnson, the FBI's position on civil rights was forced in a new direction. Johnson championed several pieces of civil rights legislation in 1964 and 1965, and he was outspoken in his criticism of the violent response to the civil rights movement in the South. The murder of three civil rights workers in Mississippi in 1964 placed even greater pressure on the FBI to oppose racial violence publicly. In July 1964, Hoover agreed to open an FBI field office in Jackson, Mississippi, and begin a counterintelligence program against the Ku Klux Klan and other racist groups.

On January 1, 1965, Hoover reached the age of 70—the mandatory age of retirement. President Johnson granted a special waiver, continued by President Richard M. Nixon, that allowed Hoover to remain at the head of the agency. Both Johnson and Nixon involved the FBI in surveillance of those critical of Vietnam War policy, including congressmen and reporters. Johnson involved the FBI in surveillance of his political opponents. Under Nixon, the FBI was involved in wiretapping members of Nixon's own White House and National Security Council (NSC) staff, as well as four reporters, to determine the source of a leak to *The New York Times*. Although the source of the leak was never uncovered, the wiretaps continued for nearly two years.

In 1970, Nixon asked the FBI to provide embarrassing personal information about members of the White House press corps. The FBI also monitored the activities of protest groups using wiretaps, bugs, and intercepted mail. Many of these activities were illegal.

FBI DIRECTORS

Throughout the FBI's history, surprisingly few men have served as its director. This is due, in part, to the astonishingly long period during which the FBI was headed by J. Edgar Hoover. The agency that these men have headed has not always been known as the FBI; their title has not always been director. But these men have served as the leaders of the nation's chief investigative agency:

Name	Title	Time in Office
Stanley Finch	Chief	1908–1912
Alexander B. Bielaski	Chief	1912–1919
William E. Allen	Acting Chief	1919
William J. Flynn	Chief	1919–1921
William J. Burns	Director	1921–1924
J. Edgar Hoover	Director	1924–1972
L. Patrick Grey	Acting Director	1972–1973
William D. Ruckelshaus	Acting Director	1973
Clarence M. Kelley	Director	1973–1978
James B. Adams	Acting Director	1978
William H. Webster	Director	1978–1987
John Otto	Acting Director	1987
William S. Sessions	Director	1987–1993
Floyd I. Clarke	Acting Director	1993
Louis Freeh	Director	1993–2001
Thomas J. Pickard	Acting Director	2001
Robert S. Mueller, III	Director	2001–present

Nixon's activities led to the Watergate scandal of 1972, and Nixon was ultimately forced to resign to avoid impeachment. As part of the Senate's and House of Representatives' investigations into Nixon's abuse of power, the FBI's wiretapping of reporters and White House and NSC staff came to light. In addition, evidence was revealed during the investigation that Hoover kept many files on public officials that contained embarrassing information about them.

In 1972, Hoover died after an astonishing 48 years as the head of the FBI. Shortly after his death, the evidence of improper conduct by the FBI led to an investigation of the type of work carried out by the FBI and the Central Intelligence Agency (CIA). By 1975, committees had been established in the House of Representatives and the Senate to determine how the FBI and the CIA had acted in the past and what reforms were needed for the future. The committees were named for their chairmen—Representative Otis Pike of New York in the House and Senator Frank Church of Idaho in the Senate.

The Pike and Church committees offered extensive recommendations about how the FBI should be revamped, given the evidence of the bureau's operations outside its traditional role. Stricter restrictions were placed on the FBI's ability to conduct domestic security operations (those that did not involve criminal investigations), and such investigations were placed under the bureau's Criminal Division, rather than the Intelligence Division. The major focus of both committees was to ensure that the

FBI could not be used by the White House to harass organizations or individuals.

REFORM AND RESURGENCE

A shift in FBI priorities toward focusing on white-collar crime (a crime committed in connection with business or professional activities) and the use of new investigative techniques like undercover work led, in the 1980s, to FBI investigations into charges of illegal activity on the part of elected figures. In the Abscam operation, FBI agents first launched an investigation into stolen securities and paintings. (The operation was named Abscam for "Abdul scam"—Abdul being the name of an imaginary sheik who was supposedly interested in purchasing stolen goods.) The investigation, however, led undercover FBI agents to approach Angelo Errichetti, the mayor of Camden, New Jersey, with a proposal for the sheik to invest in the Camden port in exchange for political favors. Under Errichetti's direction, FBI agents then approached congressmen to seek political asylum for the imaginary sheik Abdul. The agents were told that the congressional assistance would cost the sheik some $50,000. Ultimately 12 officials were convicted in the Abscam operation, including one senator and six congressmen. In a second operation, nicknamed Greylord, the corrupt officials exposed included police officers and judges in Cook County, Illinois.

FBI efforts also focused on organized crime. In the "Pizza Connection" case, FBI investigations exposed a nationwide crime ring that used pizza parlors as a cover

After the Watergate scandal of the early 1970s and the revelation that J. Edgar Hoover kept secret files on public officials, the FBI underwent several changes. Priorities shifted to white-collar crime, like the Abscam operation, which led to the conviction of one U.S. senator and six congressmen.

for drug trafficking. The FBI convicted numerous crime leaders in cities across the country, using wiretaps, undercover operations, and informants.

Under President Ronald Reagan, the FBI was given broader powers to conduct domestic security/terrorism investigations, following the Reagan administration's concern about the rise of fundamentalist Islamic movements and the Soviet Union's efforts at political expansion. Under new guidelines provided by Reagan's attorney general, William French Smith, the FBI was authorized to take a more proactive stance in domestic security, launching investigations designed to prevent a crime rather than waiting until a crime had been committed.

Even with the end of the Cold War, the FBI continued to focus on counterintelligence in the 1980s and 1990s, exposing Soviet espionage operations involving former naval officer John Walker and CIA official Aldrich Ames. The FBI also collared naval intelligence analyst Jonathan Pollard, who had been recruited by Israel to spy.

After the Gulf War in 1991, FBI agents began more intensive surveillance of Arab-American leaders and groups. This surveillance increased after the bombing of the World Trade Center in New York City in February 1993, ultimately linked to Islamic fundamentalist terrorists. In the 1993 attack, a car bomb was detonated in an underground parking garage at the World Trade Center, killing six people and injuring more than 1,000. As part of the same investigation, FBI agents discovered and were able to stop a plan to blow up the United Nations headquarters and the Lincoln and Holland tunnels (two major entry/exit points to New York City).

RUBY RIDGE AND WACO

In 1992, FBI agents were trying to arrest an anti-government activist named Randall Weaver, who was living with family members in a cabin in Ruby Ridge, Idaho. Weaver, a member of the Aryan Nation, a white supremacist group, had been arrested on charges of illegally selling weapons, but he disappeared before his trial date. U.S. marshals located Weaver in a mountain cabin and tried to arrest him. In an ensuing shootout, Weaver's 14-year-old son and a U.S. marshal were accidentally shot and killed.

The FBI's 50-member Hostage Rescue Team was called to the scene. The team's actions would later come under question, specifically concerning when and how the FBI was allowed to use deadly force. During the 10-day standoff, sharpshooters shot and wounded Weaver and his friend Kevin Harris, and killed Weaver's wife. Weaver and his three daughters eventually surrendered. Weaver and Harris were charged with the murder of the marshal but were acquitted; Weaver was also acquitted of all weapons charges. The only charge that remained was for his failure to appear in court for his trial. Ultimately, the Justice Department reached an out-of-court settlement with the Weaver family for more than $3 million, although no wrongdoing was admitted.

Several months after Ruby Ridge, the FBI was involved in another controversial standoff, this time near

Waco, Texas. A religious group known as the Branch Davidians (loosely connected to the Seventh-Day Adventists) had a compound just outside Waco, and the Bureau of Alcohol, Tobacco, and Firearms (ATF)—an agency within the Justice Department—had received information that the Branch Davidians were stockpiling illegally purchased weapons at their compound. In February 1993, ATF agents raided the compound, and in the shootout that followed, four agents and six residents

Fire engulfed the Branch Davidian compound near Waco, Texas, in April 1993 after a 51-day standoff with the FBI and other federal authorities. More than 80 people died in the fire, and the FBI came under much criticism for its handling of the crisis.

of the compound were killed and 16 ATF agents were wounded. The FBI was called in to assist.

For the next 51 days, FBI agents tried to negotiate with the Branch Davidians' leader, David Koresh, and his followers. Given the experience at Ruby Ridge, FBI agents were determined not to use deadly force unless they were directly in danger. Instead, they cut off the compound's electricity, played loud music, and surrounded the compound with more than 700 law enforcement officers.

Finally, sensing that the standoff could go on indefinitely, FBI agents inserted tear gas into the compound. Shots were fired at FBI vehicles. Tear gas was inserted for several hours until a series of fires were started by the Branch Davidians at several locations within their compound. Gunfire was then heard inside the compound. The fire quickly spread, destroying the entire compound. Koresh and some 80 members of the Branch Davidian group were killed, including 25 children.

Both Ruby Ridge and Waco sparked concern about the FBI's response to crisis situations and its use of force against citizens. A basic conflict was exposed by these incidents, a conflict that continues to haunt FBI efforts today: What limits should be placed on an agency charged with protecting American citizens?

4

THE FBI TODAY

The attacks against the United States that took place on September 11, 2001, forced a shift in FBI priorities. Director Robert S. Mueller, III, had only been in charge of the bureau since September 4. Investigations conducted after the attacks revealed that inadequate sharing of information and poor communication within the FBI and between the various intelligence agencies had contributed to the U.S. failure to prevent the attacks by the fundamentalist group al Qaeda.

Very quickly, Mueller oversaw a massive reorganization of the FBI. At the top of Mueller's list of the FBI's top 10 priorities: protecting the United States from terrorist attacks.

On its Web site, the FBI states that its mission is to "protect and defend the United States against terrorist and foreign intelligence threats, to uphold and enforce the criminal laws of the United States, and to provide leadership and criminal justice services to federal, state, municipal, and international agencies and partners." The FBI's core values are also listed online. They include: adherence to the rule of law and the rights conferred to all under the United States Constitution; integrity through everyday ethical behavior; accountability by accepting responsibility for actions and decisions and the conse- quences of actions and decisions; fairness in dealing with people; and leadership through example.

The FBI headquarters is in Washington, D.C., on Penn- sylvania Avenue in the J. Edgar Hoover Building. Here

During a news conference in May 2002, FBI Director Robert S. Mueller, III, discussed the reorganization of his agency and outlined its priorities in the wake of the September 11, 2001, attacks. Protecting the United States from terrorism became the top priority of the FBI.

is where the coordination and organization of FBI activities are carried out. The Washington headquarters serves as a central location where information is gathered and distributed to the field offices. The FBI headquarters is also the focal point for activities related to fighting terrorism—it is here that intelligence gathered by FBI agents and other intelligence agencies like the CIA and the National Security Agency (NSA) is collected, analyzed, and distributed. This intelligence may be distributed not only to FBI offices, but also to the Department of Homeland Security and to state and local law enforcement offices.

FBI management offices are located at the headquarters. All FBI priorities (such as terrorism and cybercrimes) have different divisions within the headquarters, and an assistant director is in charge of each division. The management structure operates like a pyramid, and within the headquarters is a vast network of supervisors all working to oversee programs and providing oversight for the entire country.

Under Louis Freeh, the FBI director from 1993 to 2001, some of the focus of FBI work was shifted away from the Washington headquarters to the field offices. Freeh believed that fieldwork needed to be the priority, that FBI agents should spend less time in the office and more time on the street. After the attacks of September 11, 2001, however, new director Robert Mueller refocused the FBI's mission to make fighting terrorism the chief priority. Counterterrorism work was centered in the Washington headquarters, and agents there attacked terrorist efforts from a variety of angles—including translating, interpreting intelligence, and tracking financial records.

Although the Washington headquarters is a central point for most FBI operations, a few special activities are based in satellite offices. Quantico, Virginia—the home of the FBI Academy—is also the site for the Laboratory and Investigative Technologies Divisions, which conduct more than a million forensic examinations each year and offer extensive training in forensic science. The Criminal Justice Information Services Division—the largest division within the FBI—is in Clarksburg, West Virginia. This division was created in 1992 to serve as a central repository for criminal justice information services, such as the National Crime Information Center, Uniform Crime Reporting, and Fingerprint Identification.

The bulk of FBI investigations, however, is carried out in the 56 field offices and 400 satellite offices (also known as resident agencies) throughout the United States. Each office has special agents and support personnel who are working to help prevent crimes from happening and to solve them when they do, working independently and with local law enforcement. The field offices are headed by a special agent in charge. Larger offices in Washington, New York, and Los Angeles are headed by an assistant director.

The FBI also has offices outside the United States. There are about 45 of these international field offices, which are known as Legal Attachés, or "Legats." The focus of these offices is to help solve international crimes and to prevent foreign criminals from reaching America. Agents coordinate their work with law enforcement authorities from the countries where the Legats are located. Agents working at Legats do not spy or gather intelligence in these foreign locations; their work involves joint investigations carried out through agreements with their host country.

There are more than 200 categories of federal law that, when broken, are investigated by the FBI. These include investigations of possible acts of terrorism, spying, cybercrimes, corruption by public officials, civil rights violations, organized crime, white-collar crime, major thefts, violent crimes, and crimes against children.

INTELLIGENCE OPERATIONS

The FBI uses many tools in the course of its investigations. These tools depend, of course, on the type of crime being investigated. Intelligence is one of the key tools used by FBI agents. Intelligence essentially means information gathered from a variety of sources. FBI agents might obtain intelligence from an informant, who warns them of a crime or an attack that is being planned. They might obtain intelligence from foreign sources, who warn them that a suspected terrorist has entered the United States. Intelligence can be gathered from intercepted communications or from computer research.

Intelligence is not only used to solve and prevent crimes but also to develop a more long-range strategy. FBI intelligence can help local law enforcement agencies plan for crises, can help ensure national security, and can help all intelligence services respond to suspected threats in a cohesive way.

To better understand how vital intelligence is to FBI procedures, we can first examine the path it follows through the various FBI operations. First, a specific intelligence need might be identified by the director of central intelligence, the director of the FBI, the president of the United States, the national security advisor, or the homeland security advisor. Such high-level intelligence requirements would probably involve a potential threat to U.S. security or an anticipated criminal threat. Similarly, on the local level, an FBI agent in charge or local law enforcement officials might identify a specific area in which intelligence is needed.

Once an intelligence need is identified, a plan is put into place to obtain this intelligence given FBI requirements and restrictions. The intelligence first takes the form of information, gathered through interviews, surveillance, sources, and searches. Once the information has been gathered, it has to be processed into a form that will make it useful. For example, if information has been gathered in a different language, it must be translated. If the information is in code, the code must be decrypted. The information that is gathered must be entered into a database, where it can be analyzed, compared with other information that has been accumulated, and stored.

It is through the process of analysis that the information that has been gathered can be converted into intelligence. The information in the database is analyzed and evaluated. The reliability of the information and its relevance are both considered. Once this has happened, the information can be put into context with other information that has been gathered and used to create intelligence.

Intelligence takes two forms—raw and finished. Raw intelligence is the individual pieces of information; finished intelligence takes those individual pieces and connects them in a way that creates a more complete picture. Finished intelligence also makes predictions or draws conclusions based on the picture that the raw intelligence has created.

The final step of the intelligence process involves getting the intelligence to the people who need it. The intelligence might be given to those who requested it in the first place. It might go to local law enforcement officials. It might go to the U.S. attorney general or the president. The FBI distributes intelligence in three standard formats: FBI Intelligence Assessments, FBI Intelligence Bulletins, and Intelligence Information Reports.

INFORMATION TECHNOLOGY

Criticism of the FBI in recent years has focused on its outmoded forms of communication and access to information technology. In response, the FBI has made an effort to upgrade its technology to ensure that intelligence can easily be shared by multiple offices and that communication between agents in the field is swift and effective.

The FBI has created an Investigative Data Warehouse to house terrorism-related documents and records, like photos, background information on suspected terrorists, their last known location, and their financial data. Much of this information has been given to the FBI by international sources. The warehouse stores more than 100 million pages of terrorism-related documents, which can be searched by agents and analysts.

IntelPlus is another resource that can be used to search FBI cases and records. IntelPlus was created in

Raymond McCartney, an FBI fingerprint examiner, explained the fingerprinting process to a group of high school students at the agency's Criminal Justice Information Services Division in Clarksburg, West Virginia. The FBI stores the fingerprints and criminal histories of more than 47 million people.

WHY FINGERPRINTS MATTER

★ ★ ★ ★ ★

Fingerprints provide a unique identification. The swirls and ridges that form patterns on the tips of the finger are specific to an individual and, when left at a crime scene, can be used to prove that an individual was present where the crime was committed.

Fingerprint technicians identify the patterns on your fingertips in three ways—loops, whorls, and arches. In a loop, the ridges on the fingertip enter from one side, re-curve and pass out, or tend to pass out the same side they entered. In a whorl, the ridge pattern is circular. In an arch, the ridges seem to begin on one side, rise in the center, and continue on out the opposite side.

In addition, scientists have identified other focal points that are used to make a fingerprint identification. Within each loop pattern are a core and a delta. The core is the center of the loop. The delta is a place in the loop where the ridges seem to divide or form a triangle.

1994 to serve as a database for FBI cases. Today, more than 42 million scanned photos and documents from FBI cases are stored with IntelPlus. These records can be accessed through full-text searches by field offices and FBI headquarters.

Fingerprints are a critical tool in solving crimes. Federal agents and local police forces can electronically access and match fingerprints using the FBI's Integrated Automated Fingerprint Identification System (IAFIS). The FBI maintains the largest biometric database in the world with IAFIS. (Biometrics is the measurement of unique physical

There are two or more deltas in a whorl-pattern fingerprint. The arch pattern is unique in that it has neither a delta nor a core.

A typical fingerprint card contains two sets of fingerprints. At the top are the 10 individual prints of each finger, always taken in the same order—thumb, index finger, middle finger, ring finger, and little finger. These are called "rolled" fingerprints because, when they are taken, the finger is rolled from one side of the fingernail to the other. This is done to obtain all details of the fingerprint.

At the bottom of the fingerprint card are the plain impressions. In these, the four fingers of each hand are placed at a 45-degree angle to make their prints, and then the thumbs are added. It is the rolled fingerprints that are the most useful for identification; the plain impressions are taken to ensure the correct order and accuracy of the rolled prints.

or behavioral characteristics, like fingerprints or voice patterns, especially as a way of verifying identity.) Prints were first processed through IAFIS in July 1999. Millions are now processed each month. The criminal histories and fingerprints of more than 47 million people are stored in IAFIS's Criminal Master File. Law enforcement officials can send a set of fingerprints to IAFIS and determine if there is a match with other criminal records within two hours and with any civilian records within 24 hours.

When a suspect is arrested, an impression is made of the suspect's 10 fingers to record the unique markings that make up his or her fingerprints. The fingerprints are then forwarded electronically to a state or federal agency for processing, before being sent to IAFIS.

Fingerprints might also be taken of people who apply for certain jobs or for certain kinds of licenses. These also are processed on the local, state, or federal levels before being electronically sent to IAFIS.

Besides fingerprints and criminal records, the FBI also maintains records of DNA profiles, which can be used to connect DNA records from crime scenes to known criminals. DNA found in bodily fluids, skin, or hair left at a crime scene can be used to identify a suspect. At the FBI's Combined DNA Index System (CODIS), more than 2.5 million DNA profiles from 174 labs around the country are stored in an electronic database. Using CODIS, federal, state, and local crime labs can compare DNA evidence from crime scenes to link crimes committed by the same offender and connect these crimes to those who committed them.

These are a few of the areas where technology has allowed the FBI to provide a more comprehensive service to help prevent and solve crimes. In the next chapter, we will examine in greater depth the FBI Laboratory to learn more about the FBI's role in forensic science and research, and examine what types of cases FBI agents are working to solve.

5

IN THE LABORATORY

L aboratory investigations have played a vital role in FBI work for many years. The first laboratory—known as the Technical Laboratory—was created in 1932 when the FBI was known as the United States Bureau of Investigation. The purpose of the laboratory—then and now—was to assist in the scientific and research aspects of investigative work. In those first years, laboratory work focused on analyzing firearms and handwriting.

In 1942, the laboratory became a separate division within the FBI. In 1981, the Forensic Science Research and Training Center (FSRTC), a section of the laboratory division, was established in Quantico, Virginia, at the FBI Academy. The forensic science center uses research and techniques in forensic analysis to help in analyzing data left at a crime scene. The center also offers training to state and local law enforcement in DNA analysis, hair and fiber examination, fingerprint identification, firearm identification, polygraph testing, bomb disposal, docu-

THE LABORATORY'S NEW HOME

In the new FBI laboratory complex, which opened in 2003 in Quantico, the bureau's 650 laboratory employees are spread over five floors and nearly 500,000 square feet of space. The new facility is more than double the size of the old lab, which was housed in aging quarters at the J. Edgar Hoover Building in Washington, D.C.

One feature of the new facility is that the labs are completely separate from the regular office space, allowing the scientific analysis to be conducted in a sterile environment. "We were placed in a building that was made for office work, not laboratory work," Dwight Evans, the director of the lab, said in *The Washington Post* in 2003. "This building has been specifically designed for laboratory work."

The new complex featured $25 million in new equipment. The facility includes large evidence bays, where entire tractor-trailers or airplane fuselages can be examined. There are microscopes for DNA sampling, thousands of samples of car paint to identify vehicles used in crimes, and 5,000 firearms for gun-match testing. The FBI Laboratory typically handles 8,000 to 10,000 cases a year.

The FBI's new state-of-the-art crime laboratory opened in Quantico, Virginia, in 2003. The lab's 650 employees now work in a complex that is more than double the size of the old facility.

ment examination, analysis of shoe prints and tire treads, and sketch artist skills. In 2003, the FBI moved its laboratory to a new $130 million complex on the campus of the FBI Academy.

More than one million examinations are carried out by the laboratory each year. Law enforcement agencies lacking proper forensic equipment and training can use the FBI's services free of charge. As a condition for this use, local law enforcement officials must agree to accept the lab's test results as final, even if the results were not what they had hoped. They must also agree to make the results available to the suspect.

The technology used by the laboratory at the beginning was quite simple—ultraviolet lights and a borrowed microscope. Later, the laboratory added test tubes, wax and plaster (to make impressions of tire tracks and shoe prints), a one-way glass for interviewing suspects (it looks like a mirror on one side but people in an adjoining room can see through it), and a comparison microscope. In 1933, the laboratory created a collection of weapons gathered from suspected criminals, to be used for research and comparison. Later, polygraphs (lie detectors) and other equipment were added.

CLUES ON PAPER

The FBI Laboratory is made up of several units and teams, each with its own specialty. For example, many of the crimes investigated by the FBI involve paper. This is the work of the Questioned Documents Unit, which examines and compares things like handwriting and printing, typewriting, and erasures, as well as tire treads and shoe prints. This unit studies evidence that is not only on the surface of paper but also hidden within it—like watermarks, fibers, and even the ripped edges of a torn sheet of paper, a match, or a stamp. (A watermark is a design impressed on paper while it is made; it is visible when the paper is held up to light.) The Questioned Documents Unit also researches how a document was created—whether by photocopy, fax machine, or typewriter—and maintains several databases for research: the Bank Robbery Note

File, the Anonymous Letter File, the Watermark File, the National Fraudulent Check File, and the Shoe Print File.

The Chemistry Unit takes advantage of chemical clues to help provide valuable evidence. The Chemistry Unit can, for example, gather information about particular dyes or chemicals used in bank security devices and then test clothing or documents for the presence of those chemicals. Investigators in the unit can analyze stains or markings to determine their source. They investigate claims of product tampering. They can compare plastics and paint chips with suspected sources. The Chemistry Unit maintains a

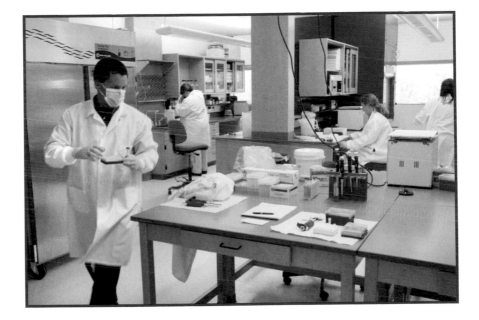

Lab workers perform the early stages of mitochondrial DNA extraction at the FBI Laboratory in Quantico. The DNA Analysis Units are among the many units and teams that are part of the laboratory.

National Automotive Paint File, which can be used to determine the make, model, and year of a car from a paint sample. The unit also handles analysis involving types of tape, caulk, and sealant gathered from a crime scene.

In addition to the DNA Index System and fingerprint work discussed in the previous chapter, the laboratory also maintains DNA Analysis Units, which analyze body fluids (like blood and saliva) recovered from a crime scene, and can also provide analysis of small quantities of DNA gathered from hair, bones, or teeth. These findings can be compared with other body fluids taken from the victim or suspect to help in solving crimes.

ON THE SCENE

Gathering evidence from a scene is often the work of the FBI Laboratory's Evidence Response Teams (ERTs). These teams include special agents and support staff—typically a team leader and seven members. Each team member has a specific responsibility to help gather evidence for a case in which the FBI has jurisdiction. One team member might serve as a photographer, another as an evidence log recorder, another as a sketch preparer. One team member would serve as an evidence custodian, another as an evidence collector. In certain cases, a team might include a bomb technician or a forensic specialist.

When FBI agents seize a computer, the laboratory's Computer Analysis and Response Team is often involved in searching the computer's files for evidence. The Computer Analysis and Response Team also assists in computer

Members of an FBI Evidence Response Team were at work on September 11, 2001, after a plane hijacked by terrorists crashed into the Pentagon. Each member of an Evidence Response Team has a specific responsibility in gathering evidence at a crime scene.

forensic analysis, which aims to find out what happened on a computer and who was responsible for it.

When an FBI case involves a bombing, the Explosives Unit is involved in examining the evidence. The Explosives Unit can gather clues from the type of explosive device used and how it was made. This unit also analyzes the residues left behind after an explosion. Finally, the unit assists in searching locations where bombs are being made or places where bombs or bomb-making equipment might be found.

WHEN A TOOL BECOMES A WEAPON

The Firearms-Toolmarks Unit specializes in evidence connected to firearms, ammunition, tools, and toolmarks. Firearms work involves evidence connected to rifles, pistols, shotguns, holsters, silencers, bullets, and cartridges. Toolmark research involves evidence left by items like scissors, screwdrivers, knives, crowbars, pliers, hammers, saws, wires, chains, locks, doorknobs, and other tools. Researchers can examine a bullet or the mark of a tool and compare it with information in their databases to determine which tool or weapon was involved in a particular crime.

Throughout its history, the FBI has battled organized crime. The Racketeering Records Analysis Unit reflects this determination to fight and ultimately shut down criminal organizations. In this unit, all evidence related to organized crime is gathered and studied—information like banking records, notebooks, tax and real estate records, computer evidence, and conversations intercepted by wiretapping. Subunits focus on gambling, drugs, money-laundering, and codes used by gang members, prison inmates, and extremist groups.

The laboratory also includes units that specialize in trace evidence found at a crime scene—like human and animal hair, fibers, fabrics, wood, ropes, and feathers—which can be used to link a suspect to a crime scene or to another individual. In a violent crime, contact between a suspect and a victim often results in the transfer of trace materials. Another unit, the Structural Design Unit, is charged with planning and designing evidence to support expert testimony during a trial. This might mean creating a small-scale model to reconstruct a crime scene or clearly demonstrate for a jury the location of evidence, victims, and witnesses. Models might also be created to help law enforcement officials in a hostage situation, by showing them a building's layout, including the location of elevators, stairs, doors, and windows. The Special Photography Unit produces, processes, and analyzes photos used in investigations.

There are units that specialize in materials and metallurgical evidence, graphics work, and audio and video evidence. One of the newest units within the laboratory is the Hazardous Materials Response Unit, created in 1996 in response to the potential use by terrorists of chemical, biological, and nuclear weapons. The unit also responds to environmental crimes.

6

IN THE FIELD

The FBI is the main investigative branch of the Department of Justice, charged with gathering and reporting evidence in criminal and civil cases where the federal government has jurisdiction. This mission comes from Title 28 of the *United States Code*, Section 533, which gives the attorney general the power to "appoint officials to detect ... crimes against the United States."

But how do the special agents detect these crimes against the United States? And what kinds of crimes does the FBI investigate?

One of the FBI's principal focuses is the ongoing fight against terrorism. The FBI's role in the war against terrorism is complex, but a key element is finding terrorist groups operating within the United States and bringing the terrorists to justice.

As part of this mission, the FBI operates roughly 100 Joint Terrorism Task Forces (JTTFs) around the country. These are groups of professionals who bring special skills to the fight against terrorism. A JTTF might include special agents from the FBI, state and local

FBI agents removed boxes of evidence in September 2002 from the safehouse of a suspected terrorist cell in Lackawanna, New York, near Buffalo. One tool the FBI uses in fighting terrorism is the Joint Terrorism Task Force, which might include FBI agents, representatives from other federal agencies, and the state and local police. About 100 of these task forces operate in cities across the United States.

law enforcement officials, and representatives from a number of other federal agencies, like the CIA and the Department of Homeland Security. Within the JTTF are experts in many fields, including linguists, analysts, and SWAT (Special Weapons and Tactics) personnel.

A JTTF is based in one of about 100 cities around the country, and its members work in that location to find out if terrorist groups might be operating there. They follow up on leads, hunt for evidence, and gather and share information with other law enforcement officials. They might help to provide security for an event in that city—a major sports competition, for example, or a similar event that would draw many people.

More than 3,700 people serve in JTTFs. The first JTTF was created in 1980 in New York City, but more than 65 of them were formed after the September 11, 2001, attacks. JTTFs have been responsible for many of the highly publicized arrests of suspected terrorists operating in the United States. They also have worked to trace the financing of terrorist operations and to combat the manufacture of fake identifications, and they also have arrested individuals involved in making explosives.

COUNTERINTELLIGENCE

Fighting efforts by other nations and organizations to spy on American soil is another priority of the FBI, as this illegally obtained information can often impact our national security. The FBI is involved in the effort to protect classified information, whether political, military, or economic.

Spying takes many different forms. It can be the pass-
ing of classified information from one individual to another, or it may be done by computer hackers or by business
competitors. It is not only foreign countries that spy, but
also terrorist groups and even American allies.

What information are they trying to obtain? These groups
often attempt to get access to classified information about
America's military plans and our efforts to protect our
national security. They are also after our intelligence—in
other words, they want to know what we know. Finally,
they may want business trade secrets—information that
helps make a particular business successful—in order to
gain an unfair advantage in the marketplace, to compete
by manufacturing the same products at lower costs, or
in the case of companies that manufacture weapons systems, to recreate the same systems.

The FBI has developed a National Strategy for Counterintelligence that focuses on five key points: keeping
weapons of mass destruction from falling into the wrong
hands; protecting the secrets of the U.S. intelligence community; protecting the secrets of the U.S. government and
its contractors; protecting U.S. critical assets (like technologies, energy sectors, banking systems, and weapons
systems); and focusing on countries and groups that pose
the greatest threat.

As part of this effort, the FBI investigates cases of trade
theft (stealing or selling a company's secrets) and providing military secrets to unauthorized personnel; efforts
to obtain information about security procedures at sites
like nuclear power plants, water treatment facilities, and

major transportation networks; and the illegal possession of classified military or security information.

CYBER-CRIMES

The FBI investigates many different types of cyber-crimes. One effort focuses on combating hackers who try to gain illegal access to computer databases and those who deliberately spread computer viruses to cripple computer systems. Another focus is on arresting predators who use the computer to meet and exploit children. Yet another focus is on targeting and arresting members of organizations that engage in Internet fraud. FBI agents also track down stolen goods sold via online auctions.

When a new computer virus is created and unleashed on computer systems, FBI agents trained in computer forensics and computer science travel around the world to determine the source of the virus and arrest the individuals responsible. By analyzing the code of a virus, these experts can learn its possible source and who might have created it, as well as its point of origin. If the virus was created outside the United States, the FBI uses its Legats and international partners to analyze the virus further, sharing information about e-mail addresses, names linked to those addresses, and other clues buried in the virus code. Local officials then have the necessary information to arrest the perpetrators.

CORRUPTION

Corruption involves cases where public officials engage in dishonest or illegal behavior, such as accepting bribes or favors if they promote a particular policy or ignore illegal actions on the part of an individual or organization. The FBI places a high priority on fighting corruption. Why is dishonesty in government so important to combat?

WORKING DOGS ★ ★ ★

Did you know that the FBI uses a team of working dogs to help with field operations? The FBI's working dogs perform a wide range of tasks, including finding people, drugs, money, and even bombs.

The working dogs are trained by a handler to perform a specific task. The handler is usually an FBI special agent, who works as the dog's partner. Because of their keen sense of smell and hearing, dogs can often find objects and people before humans can. As part of their training, the dogs are taught to perform tasks in unusual settings—for example, hunting for an object that is in a tree or in a suitcase, working in snow and in the water, or finding a person in a closet or under a pile of dirt and rubble.

The FBI uses "chemical explosives" dogs to find different types of explosive chemicals using their sense of smell. "Narcotics detection" dogs use their sense of smell to sniff out illegal drugs. "Search and rescue" dogs are brought in when a disaster—a collapsed building or an earthquake, for example—takes place. These dogs are trained to find people who are lost or buried or who have fled the scene of a crime.

Dogs trained to locate a person or an object can pick up a scent up to a half-mile away. Mornings, evenings, and cloudy days provide the best conditions for dogs to search.

Corruption makes it impossible for public officials and public offices to place their civic duties first. The dangers are clear if police officers accept bribes to ignore criminal acts. If judges accept bribes to rule a particular way in a legal matter, then they can no longer be trusted to be fair and impartial. If an inspector takes a bribe to avoid reporting building code violations, there is a higher risk that those violations might cause a fire, a collapse, or other threat to the building's occupants. A corrupt official might award a license to someone who lacks the skills to operate a particular vehicle or piece of equipment, resulting in a tragic accident. Corrupt border patrols might not adequately screen for terrorists or drug traffickers entering the country.

FBI investigators work on cases involving many types of officials in an effort to protect the public. The key tools involve cyber investigations, surveillance, the tracking of financial records, and tips from the public.

CIVIL RIGHTS

When the federal civil rights of any American are violated, the FBI is the agency responsible for investigating this violation. These civil rights include the right to vote, the right to apply for employment within the state or federal government or serve as a state or federal employee, the right to serve as a juror or a prospective juror in a state or federal court, the right to apply for admission or become a student at any public school or university, and the right to be served in any public place of business—like a hotel, restaurant, gas station, or theater. The FBI's Civil Rights Program focuses on four key areas: hate crimes, color of law/police misconduct, involuntary servitude or slavery, and freedom of access to clinic entrances.

Although a "hate crime" is traditionally defined as a crime against someone motivated by his or her religion, race, ethnicity, disability, or sexual orientation, the FBI does not currently have jurisdiction to investigate hate crimes based on a person's sexual orientation. Also, FBI hate-crime cases involving a person's disability are limited to those where a victim's housing rights have been violated. Hate crimes often involve assault, arson, or murder. Generally the FBI works with state and local law enforcement to investigate these cases.

The second category of civil rights violations that the FBI investigates involves misconduct by the police or other officials, like judges, prosecutors, and guards. These are people who act under the "color of law." This means that these individuals have a particular power given to them by a local, state, or federal agency. It is a crime for these public officials, while serving in their official capacity, to deprive someone else of the rights given to him or her by U.S. law or by the Constitution. Many of the FBI's investigations of these crimes involve excessive use of force, assaults, false arrest or fabrication of evidence, depriving people of their property, or failing to adequately protect an individual from harm.

The freedom of access to clinic entrances is a relatively new civil right, signed into law by President Bill

Clinton in 1994 after a series of violent attacks at abortion clinics. The law makes it a federal crime to prevent or threaten someone trying to gain access to this kind of clinic or to threaten or attack the clinic's staff. It is also a federal crime to damage or destroy property at these sites.

It may seem that the involuntary servitude/slavery civil right is a right that no longer need concern the FBI. In fact, there are still cases in which individuals are exploited or forced to work in difficult or dangerous conditions with no opportunity to escape. Most often, these cases involve migrant workers, immigrants, and illegal aliens who enter the United States to seek greater opportunities and then are forced into servitude and threatened with deportation should they try to escape.

ORGANIZED CRIME

For decades, the FBI has fought crime organizations that engage in illegal activities like gambling, drug smuggling, and weapons trafficking. In the same way that these crime "families" or gangs operate in an organized fashion, the FBI response is targeted to a broader level of investigation, treating these offenses not as individual crimes but instead as part of a larger pattern of criminal activity. The reason for this is simple—if a single individual, even a key figure, in these organizations is removed, the organization can still continue its criminal activities.

The most dominant of these groups is the American La Cosa Nostra (which, in Italian, means "our thing"). La

In dealing with organized crime, the FBI first tries to disrupt the organization and then tries to dismantle it. Here, at a press conference in 2002, federal officials in New York announced the indictment of 14 alleged members of the Gambino organized crime family. The chart shows members of the Gambino organization who have been convicted or indicted or have died since 1991.

Cosa Nostra, sometimes called the Mafia, is a nationwide group connected by family ties and conspiracy and is involved in pursuing criminal activities while protecting its members. Its criminal activities include murder, extortion, drug trafficking, gambling, corruption of public officials, tax schemes, and stock-trading schemes.

FBI efforts are also focused on organized crime groups whose members come from Eastern Europe and Western

Asia, as well as Eastern and Southeastern Asia and Africa. The FBI targets these groups through the Eurasian Organized Crime Unit and the Asian/African Criminal Enterprise Unit.

Under FBI definition, organized crime is any group with a specific, formal structure whose goal is to make money through illegal activities. These groups use violence or the threat of violence, bribes, and extortion, as well as corrupt public officials, to affect an entire community or region.

The FBI's goals when dealing with organized crime are first to disrupt and ultimately to dismantle these organizations. This is done using informants, wiretapping, and other forms of intelligence-gathering.

WHITE-COLLAR CRIME

"White-collar crime" refers to fraud carried out by an individual serving in business or the government. These crimes include corporate fraud, health-care fraud (including faked auto accidents), identity theft, insurance fraud, telemarketing scams, and investment fraud.

Corporate fraud cases investigated by the FBI include accounting schemes whose purpose is to cover up a business's true financial picture to deceive Wall Street analysts or investors. These cases might also include falsifying records, insider trading, kickbacks or bribes, tax cheating, and taking company property for personal use. Insider trading is the illegal use of information known only to insiders to make a profit in financial trading.

Health-care fraud may include altered medical bills, unnecessary treatments, charging for a more expensive medical procedure or service than the one provided, duplicate charges or charges for a service never provided, false or exaggerated medical disability, collecting on more than one policy for the same procedure or injury, and pharmaceutical fraud (illegally selling or manufacturing prescription drugs). The FBI targets both medical professionals who engage in illegal activities and individuals who falsely report medical conditions.

Identity theft occurs when someone illegally obtains another person's Social Security number, bank account numbers, date of birth, credit cards, or other form of identification and uses that information to get unauthorized bank accounts or credit card accounts. Identity theft can also involve the stealing of personal information in order to create a false identity for someone who wishes to conduct illegal activities under an assumed name. The FBI has targeted identity theft as one of the most dramatically growing white-collar crimes of the twenty-first century.

Insurance fraud and telemarketing scams are also growing areas of concern for the FBI. In the area of insurance fraud, FBI efforts target corporate insurance fraud, the illegal diversion of premium or policy payments, and worker's compensation fraud. In telemarketing fraud (in which the elderly form the largest group of victims), the FBI is working cooperatively with Canadian authorities (where many of the telemarketing scams originate) to ensure that criminals are prosecuted and their assets are seized.

MAJOR THEFTS AND VIOLENT CRIMES

Combating violent crimes forms an important part of the FBI's mandate to protect Americans. The FBI has developed an anti-gang strategy and an anti-gang task force to combat the roughly 30,000 violent gangs that operate in the United States today. The FBI also dedicates resources and personnel to ensuring child safety, combating kidnappings by strangers and relatives, combating crimes against children, and prosecuting parents who fail to pay child support for a child living in another state.

On the FBI's Web site is a list of the "Top 10 Fugitives." These include fugitives wanted for bank robberies, drug-related crimes, murder, crimes against the United States, and crimes against children. There is also a list of terrorists sought by the FBI, and a list of cases in which information is sought. Links to these lists may be found on the FBI's Web site at the Major Thefts and Violent Crimes page, found at www.fbi.gov/hq/majorthefts/majorthefts.htm.

The theft, looting, and fraudulent sale of artwork also involve the FBI. The agency maintains an Art Crime Team of 12 special agents charged with investigating cases of stolen artwork, and a computerized National Stolen Art File. Recent FBI art crimes have involved investigations into the theft of priceless historical artifacts from Iraqi museums and archaeological sites, the recovery of works by Renoir and Rembrandt stolen in 2000 from a museum in

J.P. Weis, special agent in charge of the FBI office in Los Angeles, talked about the recovery of *Young Parisian (center on easel)*, a painting by Renoir worth $10 million. The painting was stolen from a Swedish museum in 2000. It was recovered in Los Angeles in 2005. At left are copies of two other paintings stolen in the 2000 robbery that were subsequently found.

Sweden, the 2004 theft of Edvard Munch's famous painting *The Scream* from the Munch Museum in Norway, the 1990 theft of works by Rembrandt, Vermeer, and Manet from the Isabella Stewart Gardner Museum in Boston, and the theft of a $3 million Stradivarius violin from the New York City apartment of a noted violinist.

7

A Day in the Life of an FBI Agent

By now, you have an understanding of the full range of responsibilities handled by the FBI. You have learned a bit about its history and about the famous cases that the FBI has solved.

But what does it take to work for the FBI? What skills and talents are needed? What kind of training is involved? And what is a typical day like?

When someone is hired by the FBI to work as a special agent, he or she must first survive a challenging 17-week training program at the FBI Training Academy in Quantico, Virginia. The academy is on the U.S. Marine Corps base there; the Drug Enforcement Administration also trains employees at this location.

The academy opened at the Quantico location in the summer of 1972. The site—surrounded by 385 acres of wooded land—is private and secure. It is also extensive—in addition to the building that contains classrooms, the academy has the Forensic Science Research and Training Center, three dormitory buildings, a library, a dining hall, a chapel, a garage, administrative

FBI agent trainees take part in an exercise that simulates a vehicle stop and arrest at the FBI Training Academy in Quantico, Virginia. During the 17-week training program, prospective agents receive 643.5 hours of instruction in academics, firearms, case scenarios, and operational skills.

offices, and an auditorium that seats 1,000. There is also a large gymnasium and an outdoor track for physical tests. Plenty of opportunities for firearms training and practice are provided with an indoor firing range, eight outdoor firing ranges, four skeet ranges, and a 200-yard rifle range. There is a mock city, known as Hogan's Alley, whose replica buildings and streets are designed to provide new agent trainees with an opportunity to practice skills in a realistic setting. Finally, a 1.1-mile training track allows trainees to learn and practice defensive driving and pursuit.

The academy focuses on three main areas of training: investigative/tactical, non-investigative, and administrative. The trainees undergo 643.5 hours of instruction in academics, firearms, case scenarios, and operational skills.

TESTING THE SKILLS

To complete the academic portion of their program, the trainees must pass nine tests, scoring 85 percent or higher. The tests cover the following areas: legal (two tests), behavioral science, interviewing, ethics, basic and advanced investigative techniques (two tests), interrogation, and forensic science. Physical tests are given during the first, seventh, and fourteenth weeks of training. Trainees are tested in sit-ups, a 300-meter run, push-ups, and a 1.5-mile run.

These assessments are only the beginning of the testing, however. Trainees must pass a defensive tactics test, in which they demonstrate their skills in boxing, grappling,

An FBI instructor oversees trainees during target shooting at the FBI Training Academy. The trainees will fire 3,000 to 5,000 rounds of ammunition during their 17-week stint at the academy.

searching suspects, control holds, weapon retention, disarming, and handcuffing.

They are also tested in firearms use. Trainees must shoot with an accuracy of at least 80 percent or higher using a handgun and a shotgun and must demonstrate at least basic skills with a submachine gun. During the course of their training, the trainees fire 3,000 to 5,000 rounds of ammunition.

The trainees are also encouraged to develop and perfect their interviewing skills. In the field, agents must have strong communication skills as they work with suspects, witnesses, victims, and informants. The sample interviews

HOGAN'S ALLEY

One of the most dangerous towns in the United States can be found in Quantico, Virginia. The only bank in town is robbed at least twice a week. Drug dealers and gangsters can be found on any corner. And terrorists and criminals regularly stage attacks on the streets of tiny Hogan's Alley.

This crime wave in Hogan's Alley, though, is under the direction of the FBI. Hogan's Alley is not a real town—it is part of the FBI Training Academy, designed to prepare new FBI agents, as well as Drug Enforcement Administration recruits and state, local, and federal law enforcement trainees, for conditions they might encounter. Hogan's Alley was built in 1987, created with the help of Hollywood set designers to ensure that it had an authentic look and atmosphere. There are homes, shops, a bank, a post office, a laundromat, a hotel, a deli, a movie theater, and a pool hall. There are people on the sidewalks and traffic on the street.

By training on the authentic-looking streets of Hogan's Alley, FBI agents develop the skills they will need to function on the streets of real towns and cities. They learn how to carry out searches and make arrests, handle evidence at a crime scene, use ballistic shields for protection, and clear out an area to make sure that it is safe. They develop skills in handling firearms and learn defensive tactics.

Actors are hired to play the roles of criminals and innocent bystanders. The actors are told to resist arrest or respond in unexpected ways, helping agents develop the skills to react quickly in a variety of circumstances and dangerous situations.

that the trainees perform are videotaped, so that they can then review and critique their own performances, measuring their strengths and weaknesses.

As part of their training, the trainees are assigned a case to investigate, one that will involve the arrest of multiple suspects. The investigation, interviews, surveillance, and arrests take place in Hogan's Alley.

Throughout their 17 weeks, the trainees are evaluated by the staff to confirm that they are suited to serve as FBI special agents. Once their training is complete and they have graduated from the academy, the new agents are sent on their first assignment, generally to one of the FBI's 56 field offices.

A TYPICAL DAY

There really is no single "typical" day for an FBI agent. Given the wide range of duties that an agent performs, and the many different divisions of the FBI, a typical day can take a very different form, depending on whether an agent is in a field office or headquarters and what types of crimes the agent is investigating.

For an agent working in a smaller field office, a typical day would usually begin in the office—writing up interviews, checking e-mail, coordinating plans with other agents. Then there might be a meeting with a local law enforcement official to discuss the details of an ongoing investigation. There might be a call from local police officers that a suspect has been tracked down at a particular location, and the agent would then need to go and participate in the arrest.

Depending on the agent's field of expertise, there might be wiretapping to be coordinated or an informant to be debriefed (interrogated). Squads handling gang and drug cases do this nearly every day. Bank-fraud squads would seldom be involved in wiretapping but would spend a significant amount of time searching records. Those agents working on SWAT teams or in the violent crimes division would spend more time in a typical day pursuing suspects.

According to one agent, one way in which the reality of FBI work differs from the image we see in movies and television is that a lot more time is spent in building a case. Although there are moments when FBI agents must break down doors and engage in the dramatic arrest of suspects, those moments are preceded by plenty of time in the office, connecting the dots and putting together the pieces of a case. One key skill that an FBI agent needs is an ability to communicate, to interview people—whether the person is a suspect, a victim, a witness, or an informant.

Although special agents are given a badge and a gun when they complete their training, their skills are not taken for granted. Four times a year, special agents are tested to ensure that they still possess the necessary firearms skills.

Agents can spend months or even years putting together a case. One of the most challenging tasks any agent faces is moving from an allegation or a clue of criminal activity to proving a case and arresting the guilty person or people. The bigger the case, the more difficult it can be to develop. Each piece must be carefully thought out—an informant must be found, the tape recorder must work in a wiretapping operation, the financial records must reveal the source of criminal funding. In the end, the agents must also deal with the person behind the case, facing the individual or individuals they are responsible for sending to jail.

A CAREER IN THE FBI

If you are interested in a career in the FBI, there are a few steps you can take to prepare yourself as you complete your education. First, to work as an FBI special agent you must be an American citizen and between the ages of 23 and 37. You must be in excellent physical condition and have good vision and hearing. You must be a graduate of a four-year college. Preference is given to candidates who have also had several years of work experience, particularly in fields like law enforcement, accounting, or the military. The FBI is also seeking special agents with skills in engineering, law, science, computer science, and intelligence work. Language skills are valuable for FBI work, especially fluency in Arabic, Farsi, Chinese (all dialects), Japanese, Korean, Pashtu, Urdu, Russian, Spanish, and Vietnamese.

Before being hired, a candidate must undergo a written test, an interview, and a background check. In the background check, the FBI searches a candidate's credit record and arrest record, interviews people who know the candidate, checks his or her educational record, talks to previous employers and neighbors, and contacts any business or professional references. A special agent candidate must also take a polygraph test to confirm the accuracy of the information the candidate has supplied. Applicants who have used illegal drugs, been convicted of a felony or major misdemeanor, or fail to pass a drug-screening test will not be hired.

After undergoing the training at Quantico, special agents are assigned to one of the many field offices throughout the country. While new agents can indicate their top three desired locations, they are not guaranteed to be sent to

An arrest at an apartment building is simulated in the mock town of Hogan's Alley at the FBI Training Academy in Quantico, Virginia. By practicing in an authentic setting, the trainees develop the skills they will need to work in real towns and cities.

one of those offices. Also, new agents are almost never assigned to the location where their application was initially
processed. After three years, nearly all special agents are
assigned to one of the 15 largest field offices (if they were
not initially placed there) to ensure that all agents have
experience operating in both smaller and larger field offices. After building up seniority, agents can then indicate
a preference for their location and, when a spot in that
location becomes available, they can transfer there.

Besides hiring special agents, the FBI also hires people to serve as support staff and as intelligence analysts.
Since the attacks of September 11, 2001, there has been
a focus on expanding the FBI's intelligence staff. These
men and women are not given a badge and a gun; instead
they analyze and interpret information that is gathered
by special agents and other sources. Intelligence analysts
are typically men and women with skills in a foreign language or an expertise in counterterrorism, Islamic studies, physical sciences, computer science, engineering, or
finance and banking.

The more than 30,000 men and women who work today
for the Federal Bureau of Investigation all contribute in
some way to its mission: to protect and defend the United
States against terrorist and foreign intelligence threats, to
uphold and enforce the criminal laws of the United States,
and to provide leadership and criminal justice services to
federal, state, municipal, and international agencies and
partners. For nearly 100 years, the FBI has focused on
keeping America and Americans safe. The FBI has grown

from a small force of special agents to a large organization with offices throughout the country and around the world. The skills that its staff members possess, the scope of their responsibilities, and the types of crimes they investigate have likewise grown.

But some still question the need for a "national police force," wondering whether the FBI should be revamped or split into separate entities to combat new types of crimes, the threats of terrorist attacks, and the broad scope of intelligence demands. That this debate still exists is a reflection of the continuing challenge faced by the FBI—protecting Americans from criminal activity while respecting their rights and freedoms.

GLOSSARY

antitrust Laws and regulations designed to protect trade and commerce from unfair business practices.

bug A concealed listening device.

Cold War The ideological conflict between the United States and the Soviet Union during the second half of the twentieth century; the conflict never led to direct military action.

corruption The use of a position of trust for dishonest gain.

cyber crime A crime committed on a computer network, especially the Internet.

debrief To interrogate someone formally and systematically in order to obtain useful intelligence or information.

espionage The use of spies to obtain information about the plans and activities of a foreign government or a competing company.

extortion The crime of obtaining money or something else of value by intimidation or by the abuse of one's office or authority.

forensic science A branch of medicine used for legal purposes and concerned with determining the cause of death, the examination of injuries due to crime, and the examination of tissue sample relevant to crime.

identity theft   The illegal use of someone else's personal information (like a Social Security number) in order to obtain money or credit.

informant   A person who supplies information to the authorities.

insider trading   The illegal use of information known only to insiders to make a profit in financial trading.

intelligence   Information concerning an enemy or a potential enemy, as well as the evaluated conclusions or analysis drawn from such information.

interstate   Of, connecting, or existing between two or more states.

polygraph   An instrument used to determine if a person is telling the truth; a lie detector.

sabotage   Destructive or obstructive action taken by a civilian or an enemy agent to hinder a nation's war effort.

Secret Service   A division of the U.S. Treasury Department responsible for protection of the president and suppression of counterfeiting.

watermark   A design impressed on paper while it is made; it is visible when the paper is held up to light.

white-collar crime   Any of various crimes (like embezzlement, fraud, or theft) committed by business or professional people while working at their occupations.

wiretap   A concealed listening device used on telephone or telegraph wires to obtain information.

BIBLIOGRAPHY

Freeh, Louis J. *My FBI*. New York: St. Martin's Press, 2005.

Kessler, Ronald. *The Bureau: The Secret History of the FBI*. New York: St. Martin's Press, 2002.

Kessler, Ronald. *The FBI: Inside the World's Most Powerful Law Enforcement Agency*. New York: Pocket Books, 1994.

Powers, Richard Gid. *Secrecy and Power: The Life of J. Edgar Hoover*. New York: Free Press, 1987.

Theoharis, Athan G. *The FBI and American Democracy: A Brief Critical History*. Lawrence, Kan.: University Press of Kansas, 2004.

Theoharis, Athan G. (ed.) *The FBI: A Comprehensive Reference Guide*. Phoenix, Ariz.: The Oryx Press, 1998.

Welch, Neil J. *Inside Hoover's FBI*. Garden City, N.Y.: Doubleday, 1984.

Whitehead, Don. *The FBI Story*. New York: Random House, 1956.

Web Sites

Federal Bureau of Investigation
www.fbi.gov

Federation of American Scientists
www.fas.org

Freedom of Information-Privacy Act: Electronic Reading Room
http://foia.fbi.gov/room.htm

Internet Crime Complaint Center
www.ic3.gov

FURTHER READING

Baker, David. *CIA and FBI: Fighting Terrorism*. Vero Beach, Fla.: Rourke Publishing, 2005.

Gaines, Ann. *Special Agent and Careers in the FBI*. Berkeley Heights, N.J.: Enslow Publishers, 2006.

Keeley, Jennifer. *Deterring and Investigating Attack: The Role of the FBI and the CIA*. San Diego, Calif.: Lucent Books, 2003.

Kessler, Ronald. *The FBI: Inside the World's Most Powerful Law Enforcement Agency*. New York: Pocket Books, 1994.

Streissguth, Thomas. *J. Edgar Hoover: Powerful FBI Director*. Berkeley Heights, N.J.: Enslow Publishers, 2002.

Theoharis, Athan G. (ed.). *The FBI: A Comprehensive Reference Guide*. Phoenix, Ariz.: The Oryx Press, 1998.

Treanor, Nick (ed.). *The Waco Standoff*. San Diego, Calif.: Greenhaven Press, 2003.

Web Sites

Basics of DNA Fingerprinting
http://protist.biology.washington.edu/fingerprint/dnaintro.html

Bureau of Alcohol, Tobacco, and Firearms Kids' Page
www.atf.gov/kids/index.htm

Federal Bureau of Investigation: Kids' Page
www.fbi.gov/fbikids.htm

Freedom of Information-Privacy Act: Electronic Reading Room
http://foia.fbi.gov/room.htm

Frontline: Inside the Terror Network
www.pbs.org/wgbh/pages/frontline/shows/network/

Justice for Kids and Youth
www.usdoj.gov/kidspage

National Crime Prevention Council
www.ncpc.org/

PICTURE CREDITS

INDEX

ABOUT THE AUTHOR

HEATHER LEHR WAGNER is a writer and editor. She is the author of more than 30 books exploring social and political issues and focusing on the lives of prominent men and women. She earned a B.A. in political science from Duke University and an M.A. in government from the College of William and Mary. She lives with her husband and family in Pennsylvania.